Look at Max!

By Donna Latham

Illustrated by Ana Ochoa

Target Skill Character
Story Words *vest, must*

PEARSON

Scott
Foresman

I am Max Mox.

I am a duck.

Quack, quack, quack!

I like the black vest.

Look at the clock, Max Mox!

I can see the clock.

Max Mox must run!